᧬᠆᠆ Scripture Study Journal ᧬᠆᠆

Chapters

This Journal Belongs To

My Journal Volume

᧬᠆᠆

Date I Began this Journal

Date I Completed this Journal

∽ How to Use this Journal ∽

- This journal is meant to help you in your scripture studying of individual **CHAPTERS** and **VERSES**.
- It is designed to :
  1- Help you to organize your studies and be able to find things easily
  2- Offer you an effective way to record what you are learning
  3- Help you to reference your writings with other journals you have, or will have
  4- Help you dig and discover as you study your scriptures
- This journal focuses on studying individual **CHAPTERS** and **VERSES** (there is also a companion journal that helps you study individual **TOPICS**). The journals are similar in nature and have places where you can reference to each other.
  - For example, if you study a chapter that teaches a lot about "FAITH" and you also have a page in your TOPIC journal about "FAITH" there is a place in each journal where you can link them to each other.
  - On the first page of this journal there is a place where you can determine what "volume" this journal is. We recommend that you start this journal as volume one and the next journal as volume two, and so on.
  - When you link from journal to journal, your references can look something like: "See also Volume 1, page 24" or even easier: "1:24". Then you go to volume 1, page 24, and link *back* to the page you just wrote that reference on! Now your writings are organized and will be easy to find!
- On page 3 of this journal you have a TABLE OF CONTENTS to help you keep an organized record of where you can find the chapters that you have studied and written about.

4 – 5	Matthew 1:1–15
6–7	Matthew 1:16–25

- On each page in your journal you have various boxes with places you can record things. Here are some ways you can use those boxes:
- **WORDS I LOOKED UP**: As you come across words that you don't understand or want to know more about, look it up and write it in this box. What you have to write doesn't have to be a just a dictionary definition, it can be an insight to the word, too.
  - Example: **FAITH:**
    - Complete trust or confidence in God.
    - Faith grows as we act and feed the faith we have. Like a seed.
- **SIGNIFICANT DOCTRINES AND PRINCIPLES**: In this box you can keep a record of the various doctrines and principles in the verses you are studying. For example, while studying James 2:17, I could write:

Faith	Faith alone, without works (actions), is dead... or not alive in me. See what I DO to see how much faith I have.	2 : 26 3 : 45

The column to the far right provides you a place to link to other journals you have written about that doctrine or principle (as explained above).

- **PEOPLE IN THIS CHAPTER**: In this box you can write about the people you are reading about. You can write about the authors themselves, or the people in the stories you are reading about.
- **QUESTIONS I ASKED**: Asking questions while you study will help you gain further insights and inspiration. The questions could be about what certain phrases mean, how a certain principle applies to you, specific questions about a verse, what a scripture means that you may not understand, etc.
- **OTHER SCRIPTURES I LOOKED UP**: Here you can cross-reference to other scriptures to gain further insights.
- **INSIGHTS FROM STUDY GUIDES, ETC.**: As you study what others have said or written, you can record some of the most meaningful things here.
- **MY PERSONAL THOUGHTS AND EXPERIENCES**: In this box you can record any thoughts you have about what you are studying. You are writing your own personal commentary. This can include: things that have impressed you while studying, personal experiences, insights you have gained, personal testimony, etc. As you write about what you have learned in specific verses, you can write that verse down in the left column.
- **For more ideas and examples on how to use this journal come to www.theredheadedhostess.com**

My Table of Contents

Page Numbers	Topics

Page Numbers	Topics

Book and Chapter

Words I Looked Up

Verse	Word	Definition

Significant Doctrines and Principles I Found

Doctrine or Principle	What I learned	Other Journals

People in this Chapter

Person(s)	What I learned from them

Questions I Asked

Other Scriptures I Looked Up

Scripture	What I learned

Insights from Study Guides, Etc.

My Personal Thoughts and Insights

Verse	

Book and Chapter

Words I Looked Up

Verse	Word	Definition

Significant Doctrines and Principles I Found

Other Journals

Doctrine or Principle	What I learned	

People in this Chapter

Person(s)	What I learned from them

Questions I Asked

Other Scriptures I Looked Up

Scripture	What I learned

Insights from Study Guides, Etc.

My Personal Thoughts and Insights

Verse	

Book and Chapter

Words I Looked Up

Verse	Word	Definition

People in this Chapter

Person(s)	What I learned from them

Other Scriptures I Looked Up

Scripture	What I learned

Significant Doctrines and Principles I Found

Doctrine or Principle	What I learned	Other Journals

Questions I Asked

Insights from Study Guides, Etc.

My Personal Thoughts and Insights

Verse	

Book and Chapter

Words I Looked Up

Verse	Word	Definition

People in this Chapter

Person(s)	What I learned from them

Other Scriptures I Looked Up

Scripture	What I learned

Significant Doctrines and Principles I Found

Doctrine or Principle	What I learned	Other Journals

Questions I Asked

Insights from Study Guides, Etc.

My Personal Thoughts and Insights

Verse	

Book and Chapter

Words I Looked Up

Verse	Word	Definition

People in this Chapter

Person(s)	What I learned from them

Other Scriptures I Looked Up

Scripture	What I learned

Significant Doctrines and Principles I Found

Doctrine or Principle	What I learned	Other Journals

Questions I Asked

Insights from Study Guides, Etc.

My Personal Thoughts and Insights

Verse

Book and Chapter

Words I Looked Up

Verse	Word	Definition

People in this Chapter

Person(s)	What I learned from them

Other Scriptures I Looked Up

Scripture	What I learned

Significant Doctrines and Principles I Found

Doctrine or Principle	What I learned	Other Journals

Questions I Asked

Insights from Study Guides, Etc.

My Personal Thoughts and Insights

Verse	

Book and Chapter

Words I Looked Up

Verse	Word	Definition

Significant Doctrines and Principles I Found

Doctrine or Principle	What I learned	Other Journals

People in this Chapter

Person(s)	What I learned from them

Questions I Asked

Other Scriptures I Looked Up

Scripture	What I learned

Insights from Study Guides, Etc.

My Personal Thoughts and Insights

Verse

Book and Chapter

Words I Looked Up

Verse	Word	Definition

People in this Chapter

Person(s)	What I learned from them

Other Scriptures I Looked Up

Scripture	What I learned

Significant Doctrines and Principles I Found | Other Journals

Doctrine or Principle	What I learned	Other Journals

Questions I Asked

Insights from Study Guides, Etc.

My Personal Thoughts and Insights

Verse

Book and Chapter

Words I Looked Up

Verse	Word	Definition

Significant Doctrines and Principles I Found

Other Journals

Doctrine or Principle	What I learned	

People in this Chapter

Person(s)	What I learned from them

Questions I Asked

Other Scriptures I Looked Up

Scripture	What I learned

Insights from Study Guides, Etc.

My Personal Thoughts and Insights

Verse

Book and Chapter

Words I Looked Up

Verse	Word	Definition

Significant Doctrines and Principles I Found

Doctrine or Principle	What I learned	Other Journals

People in this Chapter

Person(s)	What I learned from them

Questions I Asked

Other Scriptures I Looked Up

Scripture	What I learned

Insights from Study Guides, Etc.

My Personal Thoughts and Insights

Verse

Book and Chapter

Words I Looked Up

Verse	Word	Definition

People in this Chapter

Person(s)	What I learned from them

Other Scriptures I Looked Up

Scripture	What I learned

Significant Doctrines and Principles I Found

Doctrine or Principle	What I learned	Other Journals

Questions I Asked

Insights from Study Guides, Etc.

My Personal Thoughts and Insights

Verse

- -
Book and Chapter

Words I Looked Up

Verse	Word	Definition

Significant Doctrines and Principles I Found

Other Journals

Doctrine or Principle	What I learned	

People in this Chapter

Person(s)	What I learned from them

Questions I Asked

Other Scriptures I Looked Up

Scripture	What I learned

Insights from Study Guides, Etc.

My Personal Thoughts and Insights

Verse	

- -
Book and Chapter

Words I Looked Up

Verse	Word	Definition

Significant Doctrines and Principles I Found

Doctrine or Principle	What I learned	Other Journals

People in this Chapter

Person(s)	What I learned from them

Questions I Asked

Other Scriptures I Looked Up

Scripture	What I learned

Insights from Study Guides, Etc.

My Personal Thoughts and Insights

Verse

Book and Chapter

Words I Looked Up

Verse	Word	Definition

Significant Doctrines and Principles I Found

Doctrine or Principle	What I learned	Other Journals

People in this Chapter

Person(s)	What I learned from them

Questions I Asked

Other Scriptures I Looked Up

Scripture	What I learned

Insights from Study Guides, Etc.

My Personal Thoughts and Insights

Verse

Book and Chapter

Words I Looked Up

Verse	Word	Definition

Significant Doctrines and Principles I Found

Other Journals

Doctrine or Principle	What I learned	

People in this Chapter

Person(s)	What I learned from them

Questions I Asked

Other Scriptures I Looked Up

Scripture	What I learned

Insights from Study Guides, Etc.

My Personal Thoughts and Insights

Verse	

Book and Chapter

Words I Looked Up

Verse	Word	Definition

Significant Doctrines and Principles I Found

Doctrine or Principle	What I learned	Other Journals

People in this Chapter

Person(s)	What I learned from them

Questions I Asked

Other Scriptures I Looked Up

Scripture	What I learned

Insights from Study Guides, Etc.

My Personal Thoughts and Insights

Verse

Book and Chapter

Words I Looked Up

Verse	Word	Definition

Significant Doctrines and Principles I Found

		Other Journals

Doctrine or Principle	What I learned

People in this Chapter

Person(s)	What I learned from them

Questions I Asked

Other Scriptures I Looked Up

Scripture	What I learned

Insights from Study Guides, Etc.

My Personal Thoughts and Insights

Verse	

Book and Chapter

Words I Looked Up

Verse	Word	Definition

Significant Doctrines and Principles I Found

Doctrine or Principle	What I learned	Other Journals

People in this Chapter

Person(s)	What I learned from them

Questions I Asked

Other Scriptures I Looked Up

Scripture	What I learned

Insights from Study Guides, Etc.

My Personal Thoughts and Insights

Verse	

Book and Chapter

Words I Looked Up

Verse	Word	Definition

Significant Doctrines and Principles I Found

Other Journals

Doctrine or Principle	What I learned	

People in this Chapter

Person(s)	What I learned from them

Questions I Asked

Other Scriptures I Looked Up

Scripture	What I learned

Insights from Study Guides, Etc.

My Personal Thoughts and Insights

Verse

Book and Chapter

Words I Looked Up

Verse	Word	Definition

Significant Doctrines and Principles I Found | Other Journals

Doctrine or Principle	What I learned	

People in this Chapter

Person(s)	What I learned from them

Questions I Asked

Other Scriptures I Looked Up

Scripture	What I learned

Insights from Study Guides, Etc.

My Personal Thoughts and Insights

Verse	

Book and Chapter

Words I Looked Up

Verse	Word	Definition

Significant Doctrines and Principles I Found

Doctrine or Principle	What I learned	Other Journals

People in this Chapter

Person(s)	What I learned from them

Questions I Asked

Other Scriptures I Looked Up

Scripture	What I learned

Insights from Study Guides, Etc.

My Personal Thoughts and Insights

Verse

Book and Chapter

Words I Looked Up

Verse	Word	Definition

Significant Doctrines and Principles I Found

Other Journals

Doctrine or Principle	What I learned	

People in this Chapter

Person(s)	What I learned from them

Questions I Asked

Other Scriptures I Looked Up

Scripture	What I learned

Insights from Study Guides, Etc.

My Personal Thoughts and Insights

Verse

Book and Chapter

Words I Looked Up

Verse	Word	Definition

Significant Doctrines and Principles I Found

Doctrine or Principle	What I learned	Other Journals

People in this Chapter

Person(s)	What I learned from them

Questions I Asked

Other Scriptures I Looked Up

Scripture	What I learned

Insights from Study Guides, Etc.

My Personal Thoughts and Insights

Verse

Book and Chapter

Words I Looked Up

Verse	Word	Definition

Significant Doctrines and Principles I Found

Doctrine or Principle	What I learned	Other Journals

People in this Chapter

Person(s)	What I learned from them

Questions I Asked

Other Scriptures I Looked Up

Scripture	What I learned

Insights from Study Guides, Etc.

My Personal Thoughts and Insights

Verse

Book and Chapter

Words I Looked Up

Verse	Word	Definition

Significant Doctrines and Principles I Found

	Other Journals

Doctrine or Principle	What I learned	

People in this Chapter

Person(s)	What I learned from them

Questions I Asked

Other Scriptures I Looked Up

Scripture	What I learned

Insights from Study Guides, Etc.

My Personal Thoughts and Insights

Verse

Book and Chapter

Words I Looked Up

Verse	Word	Definition

People in this Chapter

Person(s)	What I learned from them

Other Scriptures I Looked Up

Scripture	What I learned

Significant Doctrines and Principles I Found

Doctrine or Principle	What I learned	Other Journals

Questions I Asked

Insights from Study Guides, Etc.

My Personal Thoughts and Insights

Verse

Book and Chapter

Words I Looked Up

Verse	Word	Definition

Significant Doctrines and Principles I Found

Doctrine or Principle	What I learned	Other Journals

People in this Chapter

Person(s)	What I learned from them

Questions I Asked

Other Scriptures I Looked Up

Scripture	What I learned

Insights from Study Guides, Etc.

My Personal Thoughts and Insights

Verse	

Book and Chapter

Words I Looked Up

Verse	Word	Definition

People in this Chapter

Person(s)	What I learned from them

Other Scriptures I Looked Up

Scripture	What I learned

Significant Doctrines and Principles I Found | Other Journals

Doctrine or Principle	What I learned

Questions I Asked

Insights from Study Guides, Etc.

My Personal Thoughts and Insights

Verse	

Book and Chapter

Words I Looked Up

Verse	Word	Definition

People in this Chapter

Person(s)	What I learned from them

Other Scriptures I Looked Up

Scripture	What I learned

Significant Doctrines and Principles I Found

Doctrine or Principle	What I learned	Other Journals

Questions I Asked

Insights from Study Guides, Etc.

My Personal Thoughts and Insights

Verse

Book and Chapter

Words I Looked Up

Verse	Word	Definition

People in this Chapter

Person(s)	What I learned from them

Other Scriptures I Looked Up

Scripture	What I learned

Significant Doctrines and Principles I Found

Doctrine or Principle	What I learned	Other Journals

Questions I Asked

Insights from Study Guides, Etc.

My Personal Thoughts and Insights

Verse

Book and Chapter

Words I Looked Up

Verse	Word	Definition

People in this Chapter

Person(s)	What I learned from them

Other Scriptures I Looked Up

Scripture	What I learned

Significant Doctrines and Principles I Found

Doctrine or Principle	What I learned	Other Journals

Questions I Asked

Insights from Study Guides, Etc.

My Personal Thoughts and Insights

Verse	

Book and Chapter

Words I Looked Up

Verse	Word	Definition

Significant Doctrines and Principles I Found

Other Journals

Doctrine or Principle	What I learned	

People in this Chapter

Person(s)	What I learned from them

Questions I Asked

Other Scriptures I Looked Up

Scripture	What I learned

Insights from Study Guides, Etc.

My Personal Thoughts and Insights

Verse

Book and Chapter

Words I Looked Up

Verse	Word	Definition

Significant Doctrines and Principles I Found

Other Journals

Doctrine or Principle	What I learned

People in this Chapter

Person(s)	What I learned from them

Questions I Asked

Other Scriptures I Looked Up

Scripture	What I learned

Insights from Study Guides, Etc.

My Personal Thoughts and Insights

Verse

Book and Chapter

Words I Looked Up

Verse	Word	Definition

Significant Doctrines and Principles I Found

Doctrine or Principle	What I learned	Other Journals

People in this Chapter

Person(s)	What I learned from them

Other Scriptures I Looked Up

Scripture	What I learned

Questions I Asked

Insights from Study Guides, Etc.

My Personal Thoughts and Insights

Verse

Book and Chapter

Words I Looked Up

Verse	Word	Definition

Significant Doctrines and Principles I Found

Doctrine or Principle	What I learned

People in this Chapter

Person(s)	What I learned from them

Other Scriptures I Looked Up

Scripture	What I learned

Questions I Asked

Insights from Study Guides, Etc.

My Personal Thoughts and Insights

Verse

Book and Chapter

Words I Looked Up

Verse	Word	Definition

Significant Doctrines and Principles I Found

Other Journals

Doctrine or Principle	What I learned	

People in this Chapter

Person(s)	What I learned from them

Questions I Asked

Other Scriptures I Looked Up

Scripture	What I learned

Insights from Study Guides, Etc.

My Personal Thoughts and Insights

Verse

Book and Chapter

Words I Looked Up

Verse	Word	Definition

Significant Doctrines and Principles I Found

Doctrine or Principle	What I learned	Other Journals

People in this Chapter

Person(s)	What I learned from them

Other Scriptures I Looked Up

Scripture	What I learned

Questions I Asked

Insights from Study Guides, Etc.

My Personal Thoughts and Insights

Verse

Book and Chapter

Words I Looked Up

Verse	Word	Definition

People in this Chapter

Person(s)	What I learned from them

Other Scriptures I Looked Up

Scripture	What I learned

Significant Doctrines and Principles I Found

Other Journals

Doctrine or Principle	What I learned	

Questions I Asked

Insights from Study Guides, Etc.

My Personal Thoughts and Insights

Verse	

Book and Chapter

Words I Looked Up

Verse	Word	Definition

Significant Doctrines and Principles I Found

Other Journals

Doctrine or Principle	What I learned	

People in this Chapter

Person(s)	What I learned from them

Questions I Asked

Other Scriptures I Looked Up

Scripture	What I learned

Insights from Study Guides, Etc.

My Personal Thoughts and Insights

Verse

- -
Book and Chapter

Words I Looked Up

Verse	Word	Definition

Significant Doctrines and Principles I Found

Doctrine or Principle	What I learned	Other Journals

People in this Chapter

Person(s)	What I learned from them

Questions I Asked

Other Scriptures I Looked Up

Scripture	What I learned

Insights from Study Guides, Etc.

My Personal Thoughts and Insights

Verse	

Book and Chapter

Words I Looked Up

Verse	Word	Definition

People in this Chapter

Person(s)	What I learned from them

Other Scriptures I Looked Up

Scripture	What I learned

Significant Doctrines and Principles I Found

Doctrine or Principle	What I learned	Other Journals

Questions I Asked

Insights from Study Guides, Etc.

My Personal Thoughts and Insights

Verse

Book and Chapter

Words I Looked Up

Verse	Word	Definition

Significant Doctrines and Principles I Found

Doctrine or Principle	What I learned	Other Journals

People in this Chapter

Person(s)	What I learned from them

Questions I Asked

Other Scriptures I Looked Up

Scripture	What I learned

Insights from Study Guides, Etc.

My Personal Thoughts and Insights

Verse	

Book and Chapter

Words I Looked Up

Verse	Word	Definition

Significant Doctrines and Principles I Found

Other Journals

Doctrine or Principle	What I learned

People in this Chapter

Person(s)	What I learned from them

Questions I Asked

Other Scriptures I Looked Up

Scripture	What I learned

Insights from Study Guides, Etc.

My Personal Thoughts and Insights

Verse

Verse

- -

Book and Chapter

Words I Looked Up

Verse	Word	Definition

Significant Doctrines and Principles I Found

Other Journals

Doctrine or Principle	What I learned

People in this Chapter

Person(s)	What I learned from them

Questions I Asked

Other Scriptures I Looked Up

Scripture	What I learned

Insights from Study Guides, Etc.

My Personal Thoughts and Insights

Verse	

- -
Book and Chapter

Words I Looked Up

Verse	Word	Definition

People in this Chapter

Person(s)	What I learned from them

Other Scriptures I Looked Up

Scripture	What I learned

Significant Doctrines and Principles I Found

Other Journals

Doctrine or Principle	What I learned	

Questions I Asked

Insights from Study Guides, Etc.

My Personal Thoughts and Insights

Verse

Book and Chapter

Words I Looked Up

Verse	Word	Definition

People in this Chapter

Person(s)	What I learned from them

Other Scriptures I Looked Up

Scripture	What I learned

Significant Doctrines and Principles I Found

Doctrine or Principle	What I learned	Other Journals

Questions I Asked

Insights from Study Guides, Etc.

My Personal Thoughts and Insights

Verse

Book and Chapter

Words I Looked Up

Verse	Word	Definition

People in this Chapter

Person(s)	What I learned from them

Other Scriptures I Looked Up

Scripture	What I learned

Significant Doctrines and Principles I Found

Other Journals

Doctrine or Principle	What I learned	

Questions I Asked

Insights from Study Guides, Etc.

My Personal Thoughts and Insights

Verse

Book and Chapter

Words I Looked Up

Verse	Word	Definition

Significant Doctrines and Principles I Found

Doctrine or Principle	What I learned	Other Journals

People in this Chapter

Person(s)	What I learned from them

Questions I Asked

Other Scriptures I Looked Up

Scripture	What I learned

Insights from Study Guides, Etc.

My Personal Thoughts and Insights

Verse

Verse

Book and Chapter

Words I Looked Up

Verse	Word	Definition

Significant Doctrines and Principles I Found

Other Journals

Doctrine or Principle	What I learned	

People in this Chapter

Person(s)	What I learned from them

Questions I Asked

Other Scriptures I Looked Up

Scripture	What I learned

Insights from Study Guides, Etc.

My Personal Thoughts and Insights

Verse

Made in the USA
Lexington, KY
18 December 2011